Contents

Anne Kennedy
Foreword — v

Xiaole Zhan
Arcadiana — 1

Margo Montes de Oca
intertidal — 27

    trace fossils — 29
    paso rio — 30
    only — 31
    bajo la luna, un caballo
        de noche — 32
    sappho 21 — 34
    no good — 35
    tuatoru st — 36
    at the bay — 37
    lift / up / over / sounding — 38
    (host) — 39
    where will the spirits live — 40
    san bartolo — 42
    metamorphic — 43
    migración — 44
    photograph — 45
    apple tree bay — 46
    two trees — 47
    the pool — 48
    as inside as the eye can see — 49
    particles — 50
    soaring asleep
        falling awake — 51
    omens — 52

J. A. Vili
Poems Lost During the Void — 55

    Funding Cuts Deep — 57
    Carnival at the Point — 58
    Tulip Season — 60
    Strategic Manoeuvres — 62
    Tobruk Road — 64
    Under the Willows
        of Maybury — 65
    Jaywalking a Turtle — 66
    Moonwalker — 68
    At the Feet of a Mountain — 70
    Beside His Mountain — 71
    Sleeping with Bats — 72
    Passage Southside — 73
    My Chemical Break Up — 74
    Flutter — 75
    Returning a Gift — 76
    Mother's Rope — 77
    Road Trip to Kaipara — 78
    Ashes of Atticus — 80
    Ōrākei Sunset — 82
    Whangaparāoa Sunrise — 83
    Not for the Young — 84
    My Greatest Poems — 85
    Your Tangi — 86

Notes — 89

AUP new poets 11

Xiaole Zhan
Margo Montes de Oca
J. A. Vili

Edited and with a foreword
by Anne Kennedy

AUCKLAND
UNIVERSITY
PRESS

Foreword

The three poets whose work appears in this issue of *AUP New Poets* write in strikingly different styles – differences in structure, form, voice – and yet each calls out to us with equally compelling insistence. In Xiaole Zhan's essay-poem, layers of memory and discovery circle and build, creating deeply felt personal and political connectedness. Margo Montes de Oca collages fragments, narratives and the found poetic motifs of her literary inheritance to explore nature and being. J. A. Vili distills the legacies of loss into a lyric beauty; by mihi-ing to friends and whānau, he places poetry at the very centre of community. So although these poets could not be further apart in how they approach their craft, each is performing that remarkable literary purpose – making connections. They connect their various ideas; they connect with us, the readers. At a time when the assertion of poetry is more important than ever, the three new voices here invite us to enrich our experience of life and thought.

In 'Arcadiana', Xiaole Zhan (詹小乐) weaves memoir, myth and critical theory to tell a story of growing up in a Pākehā-Chinese family. With this work, Zhan joins a movement of mostly women writers who have taken poetry to a new place, where the personal essay and cultural theory are pieced together to form a bricolage. One of the hallmarks of this form – and arguably what makes it 'poetry' here – is its highly refined language and structure, its patterned analysis of the self in the world. Zhan's voice and vision are as powerful as any writer working in this form.

The seemingly disparate threads of Zhan's narrative are deftly connected by various means. Symbols like *water* bubble through the text: the Noah's Ark parable which pops up strangely in the young speaker's life; the 'stench of guts and stormwater' at the Chinese fish market ('3'); the '[f]loating worlds' of British composer Thomas Adès' string quartet, the eponymous *Arcadiana* ('7').

Zhan's modal mix of imagery and storytelling also acts to unify. Packed into the crots – the small chunks of prose – are vivid descriptions: 'The blood falls into the snow' ('12'). Yet Zhan pulls no punches about *what happens*: 'My Pākehā grandfather, like my Pākehā stepfather, had an unforgiving temper. When he stabbed me with his walking stick, I would run to my grandmother in tears. She would hold me in her arms and tell me he once served in a war where he used to have to kill people who looked like me' ('17').

Finally, Zhan's intricate, layered, genre-bending 'Arcadiana' tells a common world story of place and movement in a profoundly transcendent way.

Margo Montes de Oca tells of fractured journeys through constantly surprising locations in her quixotic 'intertidal'. Like Zhan, Montes de Oca's primary concern is disruption of place and its effect or fall-out. But these poems have a partly Romantic style at their heart. Montes de Oca's often-haunting montages combine rich, elemental imagery – water, light, colour – with a world of feeling: 'to step on grass and know only its greenness' ('only'). And, 'the rocks look up at you through the surface / they move too much to be asleep' ('metamorphic'). Again and again, Montes de Oca invites the reader to experience the sea, the land, and experience itself, anew.

One of Montes de Oca's hallmarks is her homage to other poets; by finding, adapting, continuing, she highlights the importance of the reader–writer transaction. Footsteps of Sappho, H.D. and others inform the poems here in fresh ways. Examples abound. The metaphysical stance of Alice Oswald pops up in Aotearoa, as, 'dream-lines the roots of the ngutu kākā / coil up against the walls / push on the ears of the earth / with their long persuasions' ('lift / up / over / sounding'). In 'migración',

Montes de Oca employs the poetic form devised by Natalie Linh Bolderston where each stanza can be read from different directions, to luminous and meaningful effect: 'flies / from méxico / like orange butterflies'. Montes de Oca's poetics and family roots combine in rhythmic, musical, visual elegances.

While Montes de Oca embraces a romantic vein and a tensile imagism, she simultaneously (like Zhan) tells it how it is: 'my grandma is sad because / her friend wants to die: she tells me this / and her eyes are the colour of the stones' ('at the bay'). The surges and returns of 'intertidal' uncover multiple revelations, sometimes deceptively so. Beneath Montes de Oca's romantic surface, experimentation and newness seethe like a powerful undercurrent.

J.A. Vili writes, in particular, about the untimely death of his wife a few years ago. These aching yet exquisite poems go beyond grief to create a sense of solace and hope for those left behind. Core to Vili's purpose are tributes to family and friends – deep gestures that reach out. Some poems tell stories of those passed: 'Her head carved by surgeons / scars the ridge of her crown' ('At the Feet of a Mountain'). Others speak directly to the subject with a sense of devotion: 'Our boy doesn't remember you / only from old photographs' ('Carnival at the Point').

In the end, these poems are not just for Vili's circle but for all of us. What makes 'Poems Lost During the Void' reach out is the close-up lyricism, the sounds, rhythms, happenings of a life. Vili writes with an intimate fusion of the specificity of his world (including the Māoritanga of his late wife) and a universality: 'Jazz Thornton's on the news this morning // is there another girl / on another bridge? // contemplating gods & flying lessons // with fractured wings / & broken wairua' ('Funding Cuts Deep').

Vili's lyric is carefully wrought. Polished elegance combines with casual-seeming tossed-off-ness. Stories are big and small: 'the broken letterbox talks to me in tongues / I try to read the broken lips of the bottles / scuffing the edges of my blue bin' ('Passage Southside'). And, 'It's a long way to go for a rugby league game / car radio can't tune into Hēnare's frequency' ('Road Trip to Kaipara'). There is memory: 'my father's taro patch, camouflaged an army of street kids / our shed, my concrete bunker surrounded by an onion mine' ('Tobruk Road').

In the construction of a life, 'Poems Lost During the Void' moves outwards from grief to show with beautiful intensity a life observed, remembered, reawakened.

These new poets, it is clear, write with skillful awareness of the various – and very distinct – literary inheritances. Yet each poet does so much more. In *Actions & Travels* (Auckland University Press, 2022), Anna Jackson asks, 'If we think of readers and writers of poetry as wholly gone up to the housetops, is revelry all the work to be done, or can the work of poetry be directed outwards, not only serving poetry as an art or a tradition, but also taking part in politics, ethics and community building?' (p. 143). The three poets here write with purpose into our everyday world.

Anne Kennedy

Montes de Oca employs the poetic form devised by Natalie Linh Bolderston where each stanza can be read from different directions, to luminous and meaningful effect: 'flies / from méxico / like orange butterflies'. Montes de Oca's poetics and family roots combine in rhythmic, musical, visual elegances.

While Montes de Oca embraces a romantic vein and a tensile imagism, she simultaneously (like Zhan) tells it how it is: 'my grandma is sad because / her friend wants to die: she tells me this / and her eyes are the colour of the stones' ('at the bay'). The surges and returns of 'intertidal' uncover multiple revelations, sometimes deceptively so. Beneath Montes de Oca's romantic surface, experimentation and newness seethe like a powerful undercurrent.

J.A. Vili writes, in particular, about the untimely death of his wife a few years ago. These aching yet exquisite poems go beyond grief to create a sense of solace and hope for those left behind. Core to Vili's purpose are tributes to family and friends – deep gestures that reach out. Some poems tell stories of those passed: 'Her head carved by surgeons / scars the ridge of her crown' ('At the Feet of a Mountain'). Others speak directly to the subject with a sense of devotion: 'Our boy doesn't remember you / only from old photographs' ('Carnival at the Point').

In the end, these poems are not just for Vili's circle but for all of us. What makes 'Poems Lost During the Void' reach out is the close-up lyricism, the sounds, rhythms, happenings of a life. Vili writes with an intimate fusion of the specificity of his world (including the Māoritanga of his late wife) and a universality: 'Jazz Thornton's on the news this morning // is there another girl / on another bridge? // contemplating gods & flying lessons // with fractured wings / & broken wairua' ('Funding Cuts Deep').

Vili's lyric is carefully wrought. Polished elegance combines with casual-seeming tossed-off-ness. Stories are big and small: 'the broken letterbox talks to me in tongues / I try to read the broken lips of the bottles / scuffing the edges of my blue bin' ('Passage Southside'). And, 'It's a long way to go for a rugby league game / car radio can't tune into Hēnare's frequency' ('Road Trip to Kaipara'). There is memory: 'my father's taro patch, camouflaged an army of street kids / our shed, my concrete bunker surrounded by an onion mine' ('Tobruk Road').

In the construction of a life, 'Poems Lost During the Void' moves outwards from grief to show with beautiful intensity a life observed, remembered, reawakened.

These new poets, it is clear, write with skillful awareness of the various – and very distinct – literary inheritances. Yet each poet does so much more. In *Actions & Travels* (Auckland University Press, 2022), Anna Jackson asks, 'If we think of readers and writers of poetry as wholly gone up to the housetops, is revelry all the work to be done, or can the work of poetry be directed outwards, not only serving poetry as an art or a tradition, but also taking part in politics, ethics and community building?' (p. 143). The three poets here write with purpose into our everyday world.

Anne Kennedy

Xiaole Zhan

Arcadiana

1.

When I was fourteen or so, my mother wanted me to volunteer in the community because she thought it would help me build character. She talked to the directors of the church where I took piano lessons, and I soon found myself teaching Sunday school without having ever attended Sunday school myself. When I brought this up as a possible issue, my mother simply told me, 宝贝, *Darling, it doesn't matter.* I bought an illustrated children's Bible. I woke up early every Sunday morning. I buckled myself in the back seat while my mother drove me to church. My fate was sealed.

2.

When? Perhaps millennia ago. A childhood in retrospect takes on some element of the myth, or perhaps the folktale. Years ago, a long time ago, when my mother had back pain she would call to me, 小乐过来给我吸背, and I would burrow my knees beside the hill of her spine. *Too much moisture in the body*, Māmā told me when the suction cups on her back bruised in blue and purple circles, oozing with yellow pus along the rim of each cup. I imagined the body as a dark cave, bones dripping stalactites, corroding canals. In childhood, pain and healing were always closely intertwined. My mother boiled bitter gooseberry leaves for me whenever I began to wheeze. The medicinal herbs at the zhōng yī throttled the air like hearsay. 太热气, my mother would say, too much heat in the body from eating dry food. Her mother, my pópo, always said, 良药苦口利于病, the more bitter the medicine, the stronger the healing.

3.

There was too much moisture in the drenched suburb I grew up in.
My childhood asthma worsened in the spring, in those humid days that
led nowhere. I remember hosed-down blood at the Chinese fish market,
the stench of guts and stormwater from the green-eyed tanks in our
garage, my Pākehā stepfather's angelfish dying with every power cut.
The red-bricked house of my childhood was adorned with oriental artefacts,
collected by my Pākehā grandfather who had once wanted to start a
museum. As a child, I once glimpsed a hand-painted breast on a shunga
ceramic in the mirror-backed cabinet of our living room. I daydreamed
our cul-de-sac was flooded with prehistoric fish like in a Ghibli movie, the
ukiyo-e ceramics shimmering and shattering in a world afloat.

4.

Noah was six hundred years old when the floodwaters came on the earth.
The rain fell for forty days and forty nights. The flood was one of the few
stories I remembered from primary school. When I brought the primary
school religious education form home for my parents to sign, my Pākehā
stepfather said, *She doesn't need all that blimmin' Jesus rubbish in her head.*
My mother replied, *Well it not bad for her.* And then she wondered aloud,
Maybe will be good for her, as if considering an extra serving of broccoli
or green beans. The earth surged with water for one hundred and fifty
days. Everything that breathed life through its nostrils died. Of course I
remembered the love and forgiveness of the Bible insisted to us as five-year-
olds, but nothing of the murderous zoological bloodied-rainbow camp of
biblical stories. While I read to nose-picking five-year-olds at Sunday school,
I wondered at the luminous bloodshed.

5.

why is religious Christmas imagery all so joyful and pleasant? where is the inherent horror of the birth of Christ? asks the user noknowshame on Tumblr. *A mother is handed her newborn child, wailing and innocent. Her hands come away sticky. Red. [. . .] Her love will not save him from suffering. Because the thing cradled in her arms is not a baby, it is a sacrifice.*

6.

And what rose from the drench? The odour of elephants after the rain. The fertile rot of living and dying things. Let me tell you a story, Marco Polo says to Kublai Khan, who does not believe everything Marco Polo says but can only continue listening with attention and curiosity. Let me set the stage for the rest of this shattered tale. A glint of breasts on a Venetian bridge like a shard of ceramic catching the light. Invisible cities afloat with pleasure. Lucius Seneca gasping from asthma. The HMS *Endeavour* with its sails raised towards the Pacific. When? *A thousand million years ago before I was born*, says Vincent Lingiari, leader of the Gurindji pastoral strike. Let me tell you a story; a lie not meant to be understood. A miracle that is both indisputable and inexplicable. A thousand million years ago before I was born Chairman Mao ordered the development of a government rubber plantation in a remote area of Guangdong that was previously uninhabited wilderness. The humid summers and hot typhoons flooded the plantation, knocking over banana trees which the children made into boats, floating through the rice fields. Māmā tells me this story over the phone from Aotearoa. I listen from a small bedroom in Naarm.

7.

Floating worlds pervade British composer Thomas Adès' depictions of the idyll in his 1994 string quartet, *Arcadiana*. Each odd-numbered movement depicts an aquatic scene; a night in Venice, a refiguration of Schubert's *Auf dem Wasser zu singen* (To sing on the water), a ship's departure from the birthplace of Venus and, in the final movement, the river Lethe; the spidery-thin strings dissipating into oblivion. The title of the quartet invokes Arcadia of classical antiquity; the pastoral utopia depicted in paintings by Nicolas Poussin and Antoine Watteau of the French baroque. Arcadia represents nostalgia for paradisiacal realms that are vanished or vanishing; myths of lost idylls. The fifth movement, *O Albion*, is a sighing paean; Albion is an archaic name for England related to the Latin *albus* meaning *white*. Allan Kozinn of the *New York Times* remarks upon the astonishing pantheon of composers gathered in *Arcadiana*, the half-submerged and fleeting evocations of Mozart, Schubert, Elgar and Wagner.

8.

As a child, I imagined heaven as a library of white pillars; worship as time spent on a Beethoven sonata. I believed in art as transcendence; I inherited it as a pantheon of blinding albescence.

9.

In 1969 my mother was born. She grew up in rural Guangdong. My pópo grew many vegetables and raised chickens for eggs and would walk to the market for soy sauce, filling glass jars from home with the dark, golden-brown liquid straight from the barrel. Meat was scarce and the slaughter of a rooster was saved only for festivals, though my mother's brother learnt to hunt small birds with makeshift slingshots and to catch snakes in the fields. As a child, my mother had a favourite rooster with a golden tail who ran to her each morning when she called. However, this animal, like all others raised, had a purpose in a world where nothing could be wasted.

10.

Sometimes a travelling movie theatre would visit, unfurling a large white cloth across a road no-one ever passed through. Films were projected onto the cloth while the entire village gathered to watch in the evening, the children sitting cross-legged in the front row. My mother particularly loved a dubbed Hindi film she can no longer remember the name of and which I cannot find. She remembers there was a heroic dog named Kelu. When her father was gifted a puppy from a neighbour in return for a favour, she decided to name the puppy Kelu also. Kelu grew up alongside my mother and she loved him dearly. Wherever she ran, he would follow.

11.

Where is the inherent horror of the Bible? The same question can be asked of modern depictions of fairytales, or of childhood. As a child, I was fascinated by the macabre world of the Brothers Grimm, the often-ruthless fairytales illustrated in dense black-and-white ink. I have always suspected that other than in old age, childhood is the closest we ever are to death. Briefly, the changing light of seasons catches our hearts off guard. Briefly, the end of each day comes to us as many individual deaths, one plus one plus one. Once a boy is beheaded into a chest of apples by his stepmother. When? *Long ago, at least two thousand years* begins *The Juniper Tree*, one of my favourite tales in childhood. One day in winter, a woman stands beneath a juniper tree peeling an apple and cuts her finger.

12.

The blood falls into the snow. The woman dies while giving birth to a boy as red as blood and as white as snow. Her bones are buried beneath the juniper tree. After being murdered by his stepmother, the boy becomes a golden bird who sings of his sorrow to the nearby village. Upon hearing the melody of the golden bird, a group of twenty millers agree to give the bird a millstone if only it sings again.

13.

Victoria Somoff explains in *On the Metahistorical Roots of the Fairytale* that the fairytale hero must have the ability to act without reasons or motives in order to comprehend an event as a miracle. Miracles in folktales preclude actions and consequences, speaking with the tongue of fate.

14.

Briefly, as children we accept the unanswerables as we do the weather, or the kindness and malice of parents.

15.

Of course I had to ask myself, *does* it matter? It puzzled me how easily my mother dismissed my trepidation of teaching at the church despite not having a religious education myself. Does it matter? It simply wasn't a question that had crossed her mind. A few months ago my mother texted me over WeChat her recollection of the story, prefacing her account with, 我 大女儿很天马行空的, *My eldest daughter is a dreamer.*

16.

What does a story matter? When I first arrived in Aotearoa with my mother as a toddler, I had hardly heard a word of English. We moved from the single bedroom where Māmā and I lived into my Pākehā stepfather's red-bricked house when I turned three. My Pākehā grandparents who lived next door in an identical red-bricked house looked after me during the day. My Pākehā grandmother was tall and always wore coiffed wigs and perfume and had the gentlest voice I had ever heard. My Pākehā grandfather read stories to me in English while I sat on his lap. What happens when we tell somebody a story? My Pākehā grandmother had a tall, long nose and would point to a portrait of Captain Cook saying that he was her great-great-great-great uncle. I would gaze up at his nostrils in wonder, believing that I too was related by blood to a great explorer.

17.

My Pākehā grandfather, like my Pākehā stepfather, had an unforgiving temper. When he stabbed me with his walking stick, I would run to my grandmother in tears. She would hold me in her arms and tell me he once served in a war where he used to have to kill people who looked like me.

18.

Sacred myth has to be discredited and to become, literally, a lie in order to acquire a poetic quality and be restructured as a fairytale, writes Victoria Somoff. I suspect there are certain stories as there are certain lies in every childhood that we do not have the option to refuse. Perhaps we catch folktales and myths as we do viruses; a cold or a flu that nestles into our blood cells. Or perhaps we inherit them, like a family nose, or a father's forehead.

19.

I told the church that I could no longer continue reading to the children at Sunday school. My mother wrote of my decision, 她天生就是一个特别认真的人, *My daughter is a very serious person by nature.* My pópo, like many elderly Chinese people, was extremely superstitious and told Māmā before I was born that I was a child swaddled into being by the goddess Guānyīn Púsà herself. I was an answer to Pópo's prayers, albeit prayers that had been for a son. What does a story matter? Perhaps in asking this question I am simply a dreamer who takes myself too seriously.

20.

Or perhaps what matters is whether you *believe* a story. Words lie, as does memory. History is selectively revised. There are certain stories built from lies that go on to become something akin to sacred myth. Deities rise from the drench. *It might be argued that no performing arts field has as intense and reverential an orientation toward historical and iconic works and figures in its past as we have within classical music,* remark musicologists Michael Stepniak and Peter Sirotin. While studying classical piano, I believed our musical heritage to be something sacred; to renounce Beethoven would be nothing short of committing deicide. I understood classical music as a yearning for a lost transcendence. It brought me as close as possible to something luminous. O Schubert. O Albion. The astonishing pantheon of composers watches from a white temple.

21.

When I'm in London, for my first few days there, all I can see really is this colonial power that is mired in nostalgia and the ways in which it continues to treat people as if they are colonised even in England itself, says Teju Cole in an interview with *Tin House*. Very few can afford a white person's nostalgia for an Arcadia which denies their existence.

22.

The fourth movement at the centre of Adès' quartet references and satirises Poussin's painting of a tomb inscribed with the text, *Et in Arcadia ego;* death is present even in Arcadia. *Mary, did you know?* asks the Tumblr user noknowshame. *That your womb was also a grave?*

23.

Even in death, certain historical figures are immortalised as gods. The death of Captain Cook is a story of becoming entangled with a myth. Let us return to the stage. The music swells to the cry of *Cook, ever honour'd, immortal shall live!* A large oil painting descends from the ceiling: Philippe Jacques de Loutherbourg's *Apotheosis of Captain Cook*. The angels Britannia and Fame carry Cook to heaven in a flurry of clouds and light. *Cook has been killed again and again, on the beach, in the theatre, on the page, but the myth of his alleged divinity lingers*, writes Anna Della Subin in *Accidental Gods: On Men Unwittingly Turned Divine*. Subin continues, *With every new death, it lives on.*

24.

According to the anthropologist Marshall Sahlins, the story begins with Cook following the script of a creation myth he could never have read. His arrival in Hawai'i coincided with the Makahiki season in honour of the god Lono, said to return during this time and temporarily seize power from the king. Sahlins, among others, claims that Cook's arrival was mistaken as the arrival of the god Lono.

25.

Europeans are massively implicated in constructing the myths of their encounters with others – and in attributing those myths to others, writes ethnographer Deborah Bird Rose. *Cook's apotheosis becomes more tangible – more true – as we spend more time talking about him over and over again*, writes poet and scholar Alice Te Punga Somerville.

26.

The anthropologist Gananath Obeyesekere comprehensively rebuts the narrative advanced by Sahlins in Obeyesekere's book *The Apotheosis of Captain Cook*. Deborah Bird Rose writes of his book, *Obeyesekere peels away layers of mythmaking; he shows the European passion for concealing terror*.

27.

Alice Te Punga Somerville's *Two Hundred and Fifty Ways to Start an Essay on Captain Cook* was first published as an essay in 2019, in time for the 250th anniversary of Cook's arrival in Aotearoa in 1769. However, the version of Te Punga Somerville's essay I read now in the form of a book was published in 2020, in time for the 250th anniversary of Cook's arrival in the land known today as Australia and claimed by British settlers under the genocidal legal lie of *terra nullius* – no-one's land.

28.

Te Punga Somerville asks, *What's in a number?* Where does a story begin and end? In 1769 and 2019 in Aotearoa? Or in 1770 and 2020 in so-called Australia? Te Punga Somerville writes, *Time and place are never really disentangled*. I find my own words entangling with hers in interesting ways. Both our essays are structured in numbered fragments (and someone in my writing group remarks on how the numbered fragments are – unintentionally and coincidentally – like Bible verses). In 2019, I was finishing my last year of high school in Tāmaki Makaurau; in 2020, I had moved to Naarm for university. Te Punga Somerville reflects that her essay is in many ways about *the many ways an apparently singular story might be told depending on where you start. (Or is that depending on where you stand?)*

29.

After two Hawaiian chiefs were killed and Cook took the king Kalaniʻōpuʻu hostage, hundreds fell upon Cook and his men with clubs and daggers. Seeing that Cook was the captain of two large ships, the Hawaiian priests accorded his body the traditional rituals for a high chief; his body was dismembered, his flesh roasted, and his bones put into a sennit casket.

30.

I remember my serene indifference to the death of my Pākehā grandfather.
My Pākehā grandmother told me years later that she was glad he was dead.
He would stalk her on the sidewalk, following her in the family car when
she left the house. I don't remember hating or loving my Pākehā grandfather;
I remember his cruelty and his favour passing day by day like the weather.

31.

I have set my bow in the cloud, said God to Noah after the flood. *Never
again will all life be cut off by the waters of a flood; never again will there
be a flood to destroy the earth.* The Hebrew term for bow (קשת; qeshet) can
refer to both a rainbow and the bow wielded by an archer in war.

32.

In childhood, pain and love were always closely intertwined. My Pākehā
grandfather taught me to write my name in English. He sat by me at the
keyboard and taught me to pick out melodies by ear. I remember the yellow
of his urostomy pouch as he was dying. *For my brown eyed Chinese girl*,
I read from his cursive handwriting on yellowed paper years later. I grew
up unable to read or write Chinese characters.

33.

My Pākehā stepfather had an unpredictable temper. Sometimes as a child
I would sit on his large belly while he scrolled on the computer, waiting
for Māmā to come home from work late at night and chatting to him idly for
hours. Other times, he would pound on my bedroom door for taking a mint
slice from his pantry stash without asking. I would desperately strain to
hold my bedroom door shut with my back, my heels pressed white against
the foot of my bed.

34.

I have grown to become suspicious of the word mercy; for the unequal power dynamic that it implies, for the implicit capacity to inflict suffering. I wonder if mercy is only the forearm of cruelty hovering above us like a cloud, or a god.

35.

What remains submerged in the drench? My Pākehā stepfather installed a small aquarium in my room one year as a birthday present. I couldn't stop the fish from dying. My Pākehā grandmother scooped them out for me, one by one. I was terrified of the hovering corpses, the small bodies that would rise to the surface. The childhood fear is still burrowed in my chest, somewhere in the dark cave of my body. The corpses still drift along the canals that wind along my spine.

36.

Too much moisture in your airways, the doctor tutted as I wheezed in and out like a dusty accordion. *The worst wheezing I have heard in years.* My mother frowned in the corner, suspicious of the Western drugs I had been prescribed. My inhaler gathered dust in a drawer in her room.

37.

What remains in the drench? I splutter through the miasmic memorylands until I reach my Pākehā grandfather's unbuilt museum, a sunken cathedral where the dead fish rise like awful angels. A Chinese gong is struck to signal my arrival. My Pākehā grandmother greets me at the gate and tells me about an ad she saw between episodes of *Border Patrol* that will help me get rid of my Chinese eyes. She smiles at me. *You are so beautiful*, she says. *You look so different from those other Chinese. You glow.* The sculpture of a zodiac snake that I accidentally decapitated as a child nods to me, the tape around its neck rustling.

38.

After the stepmother beheaded the boy who was as red as blood, she chopped him into pieces, put him into a pot and cooked him into a stew. *How delicious!* exclaimed the boy's blissfully ignorant father at the dinner table. The boy's sister sat weeping into her stew so that it did not need any salt. However, the golden bird returned with a millstone around his neck. The stepmother exited the house in anger upon hearing his song. The golden bird released the millstone, and the stepmother was crushed to death.

39.

After Cook's body was accorded the traditional ritual for a high chief, two Lono priests presented Cook's hands and buttocks wrapped in ceremonial kapa cloth to the surviving men on the ship. The men were horrified and exclaimed, *Good god! Did you eat him?* The Lono priests were shocked themselves, countering, *Why? Is that what you do? Do you eat your dead?*

40.

Te Punga Somerville writes that some say that Cook was instead fed to a dog, which was then fed to other dogs: *A dog-eat-dog world indeed.*

41.

I call my mother from my room in Naarm. *But isn't that barbaric?* I exclaim in shock and disgust. *Weren't you angry?* My mother explains that it was simply what was done at the time. *That was always the plan. We have different way to do things back then.* Every resource was put towards survival; every animal that was raised had its purpose and its fate. *You do not understand. Everybody poor. Nobody feed animal just for play. I wasn't angry. But I was very sad.*

42.

What does a story matter? I held Māmā's hand by my ear as we walked through the Chinese fish market, the hosed-down blood seeping through my sandals and into my socks. We walked past bodies of dead fish, gaping eyeballs. We walked through the market to the zhōng yī where my mother spoke to the elderly man at the counter, telling him of my asthma. When I saw the crocodile corpse packed in ice, I wept. 宝贝, *Darling*, Māmā consoled me, *don't worry. It's not for you. I promise.*

43.

There are certain lies in every childhood that we do not have the option to refuse. In the drench, there is an empty room where I see myself opening a drawer over and over to a photograph of my dead father. It is the first time I learn of my father's existence. It is the first time I see his face; his forehead which resembles my own. Years later, my mother would tell me of how he stalked her at the school where she taught, watching her through the window of the classroom. Māmā left China for Aotearoa after I was born, fearing for her safety and dreaming of a new start. In one of the photographs, my father smiles beside my eldest cousin, prized grandchild of Pópo because he is the only boy among us. Māmā tells me that when my cousin was young, he would follow her like a puppy, praising her pale skin and thin wrists and cooing to her, *Aunty, you are fair as a fairy.*

44.

In the drench, there is an empty room where my mother shakes her head as she describes the way I would scream as a child, how once the white neighbours in our cul-de-sac called our landline with concern after hearing my cries from not wanting to wake up for school. 像杀猪, *like slaughtering pigs*, Māmā would say.

45.

In the drench, my Pākehā stepfather thrashes after me for stealing his food. I run to my room with my back against the door as it thumps against my spine. *You pig*, he bellows. *You fucking pig.*

46.

When my eldest cousin was seven days old, a pig was slaughtered outside the house window. Born in the year of the pig, he soon fell into a deadly illness. His stomach was bloated. The swell receded only after receiving herbal medication from the local witch doctor.

47.

You better tell your mum not to bring that nasty stuff into the country, my Pākehā grandmother says idly over an episode of *Border Patrol*.

48.

In the drench, there is an empty room flickering with the light of a box television. On the screen, an elderly Chinese woman's herbs are confiscated as she shakes her head, unable to understand the police officer demanding, *What is this? What is wrong with you? What are you doing? What are you?*

                                                                                 Where –

49.

do you stand within a story? I grew up believing I was a blood descendent of Captain Cook, his presence seeping through my childhood like threads of red through a hangnail.

50.

You're in New Zealand now girl, speak English. My Pākehā stepfather thumps his fist hard on the table as Māmā and I chatter in the kitchen.

51.

When? *A thousand million years ago before I was born*, says Vincent Lingiari, *Captain Cook sailed out from big England and started shooting all my people.*

52.

If I were to follow the thread as if peeling a string of skin from the very beginning to the very end, would I finally be able to see myself reflected clearly in the dark lake of my own blood?

53.

Of course I swallowed the crocodile stew; Māmā had handed me a lie I did not have the option to refuse.

54.

My eldest daughter is a dreamer, Māmā wrote in her story about me. She shook her head in amusement at my refusal to simply read a few stories to children every Sunday morning.

55.

Perhaps a story matters less in a childhood drenched with stormwater and superstition. Perhaps a lie matters less when you come into the world owing.

56.

My mother was the dux of her village school and went on to gain attendance to the prestigious Zhongshan University where she completed a master's degree in chemistry. She worked as a junior high school chemistry teacher, using her income to buy her first house. Māmā sold everything she owned to move to Aotearoa with me, borrowing money from her elder sister and filing her immigration application Christmas Eve of 2002, days before the 2003 Immigration Amendment Act would have denied her application.
In Aotearoa, she survived on minimum-wage jobs and welfare payments as she worked, studied and looked after me in a single room with green walls.

57.

Perhaps a secret matters less when it is the price of peace; when to suffer is to beg for what you cannot afford. When her hands come away sticky, bloodied with care. When she would offer anything but you in her arms.

58.

Perhaps Māmā saw in my refusal, and her own refusal of her past, the ability to dream.

59.

I used to dream at the piano. I loved Mozart, Schubert, Elgar. Beethoven. My lone, luminous geniuses, glowing and weeping like a tangle of angels. Sometimes I think I can hear in the slow, lonely subject of a fugue the sound of time before I was born. The subject of a fugue is weighted with destiny; it carries the uncanny sound of somehow being in the shade of the future slanting backward in time; like the shadows in a de Chirico painting. You can hear the structure of the rest of the fugue from the very beginning in a way that is chilling and godly.

60.

How can you disentangle worship from colonialism? I mistype 'witness' as 'whiteness' and remember Cook in a flurry of clouds and light. I remember how during a discussion on decolonising classical music pedagogy, every argument was prefaced with, *We're not trying to get rid of Beethoven, but* . . . as if to entertain the possibility of a Beethoven-less curriculum was a form of blasphemy. I remember how my music history tutor commented that my use of the phrase 'white status quo' was 'a loaded statement' and asked whether I 'worry about the relatability' of my research on Chinese-Australian composers while nodding approvingly and unquestioningly at my classmate's research into seventeenth-century trombone organology.

61.

It occurs to me that 2020 was also the 250th anniversary of the birth of Beethoven. Cook and Beethoven; emblems of empire aligning as if constellations upon a flag.

62.

What to make of the whiteness – I mean the *wetness* of Adès' depictions of Arcadia? While workshopping this essay, my classmate Anima Adjepong remarks that the wetness here is not only water; it is the drench; it is the flood. *And water is not only water*, says Adjepong. *Water is memory. Water is blood. Water is the root of colonialism.*

63.

In the drench, there is a room where my Pākehā grandfather waits beside an upright piano covered in dust. His eyes are milky with illness. Lucius Seneca crouches in the corner, wheezing in and out. The piano has outlived the axe, and the tree, and both men in the room. Like the word heaven.

64.

In the drench, there is a room where I am five, or six, reading aloud in English from a Disney adaptation picture book of *Snow White and the Seven Dwarfs*. Māmā is filming me and narrates over the top in Mandarin saying, *Every night, Māmā and Xiǎo Lè read together. Usually, Xiǎo Lè reads a story in English and Māmā reads a story in Mandarin.* In the recording, I breathlessly mispronounce the word ebony: . . . *and hair as black as albany*. O Albion. When Te Punga Somerville reads to her nephew from the picture book *Horeta and the Waka*, she thinks to herself, *Cook is the reason that you my dear nephew are the first one in a few generations in our whānau to speak Māori*. Māmā continues to narrate in Mandarin as she films me reading, *The teachers at school say that Xiǎo Lè is doing very well in reading and writing.*

65.

Any event can appear as a miracle if it is simultaneously understood as being indisputable and at the same time *inexplicable*, writes Victoria Somoff. She goes on to argue that a fairytale miracle can only be perceived in the realm of the fairytale itself, using the example of a reward bestowed upon a fairytale hero after offering an eagle food: *No individual is able to hold contradictory views: comprehending the wealth that follows as both obvious and impossible* at the same time.

66.

The fairytale is a story not able to be understood on its own terms, at least in our world.

67.

The word asthma comes from the Greek *azein* meaning *breathe hard*. However, Seneca preferred to use the nickname coined by Ancient Roman doctors; *rehearsing death*. Those who are asthmatic gasp as if constantly at one's last breath. Eventually the illness will permanently perform what it has been practising for so long. Seneca declared asthma the worst of the ailments he had experienced. However, he is stoic regarding his suffering, speaking to Death (in a translation by John D'Agata), *So, you're having another go at me. Well, go ahead! Come and get me! I had my own go at you long ago!*

68.

When? Seneca anticipates the reader's incredulity and answers, *Back before I was born. Death, you see, is just a state of unbeing. And we have all experienced that while waiting for life to start.*

69.

Rehearsing death puts me in mind of Tupaia, the Tahitian navigator, polymath and priest who accompanied Cook aboard the HMS *Endeavour*. Tupaia is today identified as the artist of the significant watercolour *Dancing Girl and Chief Mourner, Otaheite*. The watercolour depicts the traditional costume of the Tahitian *heva* mourning rite involving song, dance and rampage. There is music within mourning; mourning within music; to re-hearse is to rake the earth over and over for new life and for death.

70.

do you guys think jesus, the son of a carpenter, smelt the wood of the cross & temporarily thought of home, writes the Tumblr user katabasis.

71.

In another room, I am crouched in the dark, the glow of a laptop on my face. I am watching a VHS tape uploaded on YouTube as *Fresno Poets Archive 12 – Li-Young Lee* where the poet speaks before a reading of his poem *Braiding*.

72.

…if you look at the poem like that, see the line breaks; that's a score, like a musical score for the human voice, but because it is a musical score for the human voice, and all voice is performed with the exhaled breath, all voice is possible because of the dying breath. So it's a score for your own dying.

73.

I am constantly struck by the sorrow, suffering and bloodiness braided within the sacred. There is physicality and yearning in the story of Jesus living and suffering as a human being that cannot be ignored; Judas betrays Jesus with a kiss, the beloved disciple John lies intimately against Jesus' chest during the last supper; his followers continue to consume his flesh and drink his blood.

74.

Sometimes I wonder if the yearning is less about heaven than it is about living as flesh and blood. I, too, long for Arcadia. I, too, am human.

75.

From the YouTube video, Li-Young Lee continues to speak, *What is interesting and important about the exhaling breath is that meaning can only be divulged if we exhale . . . Meaning grows in opposite ratio to vitality . . . I think that's why writing is so fated with a tragic quality. Because the minute you start writing, you know your medium is the dying breath.*

76.

Let me tell you a story; a lie not able to be understood. What do words matter in the wake of our constant dying? In our constant rehearsal of death? There is a dark, unbuilt house in the cave of my body where I wander through my Pākehā grandfather's museum that never came to be, the oriental artefacts that haunted the red-bricked house I grew up in. I walk hand-in-hand with the letters of the alphabet that my Pākehā grandfather taught me as a child, with the ghost of my father. I think that's why writing is so fated with a tragic quality; in writing, I can only hope to be misled in ways that matter. In writing of dog-flesh, and god-flesh, and the miasmic memorylands of the drenched suburb I grew up in, I wonder if I can only ever betray myself as a lost, water-logged orientalist of my own childhood.

77.

What does anything matter in the wake of our constant dying? I am always searching for clues; conspiracies; voices small and green. *Apophenia* describes the tendency to perceive a connection or meaningful pattern between unrelated things; though, of course, to simultaneously believe something to be both unrelated and meaningfully connected is to commit a miracle that can only exist within a fairytale; let me

tell you a story. I am there again, a thousand million years ago, rocking with my knees to my teeth on the kitchen floor; the linoleum cold against my soles; I am the shape of an egg, or a poem, or a child, or an echo within a piano; I am afraid of sleeping alone; I am waiting for Māmā to finish calling Pópo from the landline tethered to the kitchen wall; she has brought a chair to the wall where the coil is like an umbilical cord; she reaches out her hand for me to hold;

the lights are on; we have forgotten to draw the curtains;

the windows face the street; an aquarium,

glowing

like a church of glass, or the lives of ordinary people;

let me tell you a story, Marco Polo says to Kublai Khan, who does not believe everything Marco Polo says, but can only continue listening with attention and curiosity;

I continue listening; I listen from a room in Naarm as Māmā tells me a story over the phone from Aotearoa about her childhood in Guangdong;

I listen; I dream; I hurt closer towards something vanishing and luminous

Margo Montes de Oca

intertidal

The dreams were not confined to her indeed, but went from one brain to another. They all dreamt of each other that night, as was natural, considering how thin the partitions were between them, and how strangely they had been lifted off the earth to sit next each other in mid-ocean.

Virginia Woolf, *The Voyage Out*

trace fossils

in the intertidal zone / anemones sleep / kelp lies in golden tongues / under black pools / in the intertidal zone / i cling to a rock / the barnacles press into my palms / imprint themselves on me / like disappearing stars / in texas this year drought scorched up a river / they found footprints in its bed that were one hundred million years old / vanished bodies shored up and shining / yesterday i saw a woman hurrying across the street / the wind swept her hair into question marks / she carried a white placard / THE CLOCK IS TICKING / i burrow into the crevices / i cluster with the snails / they write important messages on my skin / we are waiting for the water / to sluice away the drying sun / in the intertidal zone / it is always a matter of time.

paso rio
    for Trini

I dive into the river a rush of silver
there go the pink ribbon-flowers falling on the shivering
impulse of the water there goes the wind spinning
on its reflection there goes the not-yet-
actual there goes space charged
with time there goes the leg of my brother
kicking up into the volumes of light

    in a rebozo / a softness extended from you abuela /
    speaking no language but breath

behind us the swaddled river's daughter
slip-shape walks along the clay
eyes half-shut to the morning

behind us next sunday bends
strands of summer around its fingers
thrums out its impressions of joy

    siempre te encuentro / in the side-long look of dreams /
    como la sombra del sueño

in the shade of the current there go
the bed-stones all jade and tumbling like they do
in the blaze of the mantle there goes my hand
flashing down to catch one there go the glimpses
faster than a timelapse there goes San Bartolo there goes
my name out towards the sea with the river-script
there goes yours rushing past to meet it

    you loved the blue-green of this place / your face a smudge
    in the plane window / flying home

only

to forget the names of the world
to step on grass and know only its greenness
to bend towards water   and know only its mirror-shine
the name of me could be the same as the name of   anything else   you are
known to me only as the one   who kisses me   in the secret places
the one who cleans   meticulous   all the soup from the bowl   the one
who stoops to photograph   the other one   the one under the tree   spore-ripe
and round   bright as   an apple   which itself   is only brightness

bajo la luna, un caballo de noche
a glosa with Louise Glück

*

I rode to meet you: dreams
like living beings swarmed around me
and the moon on my right side
followed me, burning.

I return to that old soil in
all kinds of weather. Once,
in winter, on the road
past maize-fields and shadow,
I saw a chestnut horse tied up
to a fence, unfamiliar. Moonbeams
for eyes. Something possessed me
there, sweating cold, to swing up
towards him and so past the streams
I rode to meet you: dreams

are good like that. I saw three ghosts
on the way, clothed in flowers. One
knew all my names, said them properly,
touched the horse and left a trace,
powder-white, on its chest. Sang
through its hide like a turning key,
through its blood like a whisper.
I felt it enter my body, the ghost-chalk,
felt the world in sudden relief, memories
like living beings swarmed around me

and the dead moving again. Didn't rush ahead
like usual, on the road to Jocotitlán. Instead
they walked with me, their breath rising
almost invisibly, like spores, in rivers
to the sky. The wind another language,
translating. The curving path, a tide
ebbing towards home. Though others
had forgotten the way, I knew it now –
the first ghost on my left, a guide,
and the moon on my right side

pulsing with light. Distance folded
into itself, and currents of time
built worlds in each corner of vision. Slowly
the stars led us through the gate,
past snakeskins, past Guadalupe
and her bowl of leaves. Past returning, now,
and future too, towards that blue circle-room
we moved under winterlight. At the doorstep
they looked at me – then yearning
followed me, burning.

sappho 21

[
[
pity her
in *trembling* light
flesh by now old age　gleaming new
she　　　covers her eyes to the wind
　　　　　　flies in pursuit of
noble ruin
spills into the gold　hollow places
taking up in armfuls the　threadbare sun
let her *sing to us*　　still unknown is she　reaching always for
the one with violets in her lap
who is *mostly* arrival
and then　　sweetly
goes astray

[

no good

in the morning her hands stretch past you   into noon

                                          arranges words   into   secret gestures

    says something but then away she goes   setting off into quiet drift

it's like finding a lost thing   after twenty thousand years

      sitting still in bone-webs of graphite   a half-hewn shiver of surface

half-dipped in age   hello she says and then as soon as you look at her gone

      eddies back down into the hackles of rock   (yes   this mud   keeps well)

      into places where birdcalls play backwards   secrets open on the C horizon

and time leans downhill   while you search for her   like you're reading

      or swimming eyes shut underwater   to pluck a starfish from the floor

                                                                of a flooded house

tuatoru st

back through haunted wood   back to the crayon-smudges
on buttercream walls the kitchen with fruit in the windows
the creaking pōhutukawa dropping down against the sand

quiet the night   quiet the footsteps in the empty hallway
two boys from decades ago & their mother calling
                    (the priest came and then they left)

still the wardrobe smells the same   (still the green light
falls in a line across the floor)   &   the sharp edge of the bookshelf
is to be avoided   &   the room around the corner

crouches in blueness   pulls me with strings
invisibly felted to my skin   pulling   with oceanic strength
towards i have never known what before i wake

at the bay

my grandma is sad,
so i take her to the beach:
i cover her in pebbles warmed by the sun.
i work quietly

using a mussel shell to scoop them up
and pour them on her back,
making sure to take only the top layer,
the lip of the shell skimming over
cold wet ones underneath
where the sea is still sucking away at them.

the stones are greywacke & perfectly smooth.
some have white shot through them
like cream. when i get
to the nape of her neck
a tiny one falls into her ear
and i pick it out carefully,
and only the pink circles on the tops of her heels
are showing now. a gull is keening.
my grandma is sad because
her friend wants to die: she tells me this
and her eyes are the colour of the stones

which are hot with the afternoon.
i want her to imagine the beach
pulling her to its centre –
to picture herself a stream of water
moving down through millions of pebbles
echoing with the small noises of arrival.

lift / up / over / sounding
    after Alice Oswald

dream-lines the roots of the ngutu kākā
coil up against the walls   push on the ears of the earth
with their long persuasions   ....

mirror my hand on the photo album
looking for traces of fingers   since lifted to let in the years
like the sea dilating   when all the green rushes in   ...   .

moon-shadows the currents in the harbour
circle the throat of a shipwreck   auē qué lástima
dissolving under the waterlid ...   .

mirror your future footprints all silver-
sunkenly walking beneath me   & here and there
the fading grace notes   of the song you always sing   ...

                                                    ..
                                ....

(host)

empty   quartz   **parking**   *deposit*   **lot**

a   **busy**   *sand*   **street**   *dune*

recent   *cliff-side*   **housing**   *nest*   **development**   *of clay*

a   **museum of**   *blackening*   **dinosaurs & the prehistoric**   *swamp*

tarseal   *unmined*   **hisses**   *steadfast*   **with engine-cold**   *darkness*

seashells   **power-lines**   *fossilise*   **between**   *upstream*   **streetlamps**

billboard   *clawed-at*   **peels to reveal**   *pūriri bark*   **someone's face**   *healing over*

eyes   **flickering**   *fasten on*   **candlelight**   *berries*   **in wine glasses**

the sound of   *twenty*   **three**   *pterodactyl*   **skybound**   *wings*   **planes**   *uplifting*

communities of   **upstairs**   *ancient*   **venues for**   *bryophyte*   **music**

late-night   *beginnings*   **gallery**   *of*   **opening**   *bloodlines*

tree roots   **fingers**   *reaching for*   **reaching for**   *spring rain*   **a wrist**

where will the spirits live

1.

in the altered dream where a tree drips her white-silver
down into the cupped hands of a bucket – where like tears
it gathers, spiles drawing up her being, blood
coming off on the fingers of the waning forest.
notice the soil recording all of this. notice the red
soil watching the rubber-bark cry out all its holding.

2.

standing very still in time's great holding
is a man, covered in rubber-paint, white-silver
clinging, flooding off his body which is almost as red
as the soil. it makes handprints on his belly, it tears
off in crescent-shaped pieces and falls back to the forest
floor, back to history's oldest and most patient blood –

3.

– the earth, that tectonic tide of blood
stripped back to darkness, which holds and is holding
us all, trees, time, resistance, the man, the forest.
everything the earth makes is memory, white-silver,
sometimes future. like the crepuscular tears
of the rubber-tree. like the green inside the red.

4.

inside the soul of the green land: red,
ruby, a piece of it, hanging like a pearl of clay or blood
hooked to the rim of the harvest-fields. even the tears

on the ravaged plantation can't stop it holding
its peace there, with its halo of white-silver,
watched by the shades of sky and forest.

5.

repeating, returning. deep in the spectral forest,
the man pours rubber, silent, and the red
of the listening soil is almost white-silver
with its ghosts, as he reminds them of their old blood.
the sinew and curve of his body is its own kind of holding
for their memories, and their language, and their tears.

6.

sleeping at last in the avenues of tears,
in the avenues of the crop lines, the forest
curls up around the length of the man, holding
him close. one by one the rubber-trees with their red
bark, their tall bodies, their quiet blood
move him into the afterwards, into the past, glowing white-silver.

here, in the world's holding. my ancestors made rubber from the latex tears
of trees too, white-silver. in the sweat of the mexican forest
they found the ghost inside the red: they called it olli, or kik, which meant blood.

san bartolo

my placenta is buried there –
i visit it on google earth sometimes
a satellite image   greener than i remember.
gullies carved in wrinkles and
dust blushing down its slopes,
my dna seeping into
its soil horizons.
i reach out to it with my mind but
handfuls of orange mist throw themselves
back at me. there are birds there
whose songs i don't know.
there is an old language
which flashes open some days
under my tongue like a marigold
then closes and moves back
into the throat of memory.

metamorphic

hardened and simplified   on you swim   decapitated by reflection

    your half-human face   looking around at a world not water   but the water

is where you live now   your circulatory system is well aware   it has slowed

right down   fish-style   the rocks look up at you through the surface

    they move too much to be asleep   they want to be stroked like dogs

you wonder what it would be like   seething   sinking

    into the sediment   (tough luck)   (you're a rock now)

off to a volcano   riding some ancient tectonic tide   then whoosh!

up you'd go   igneous again   lashing yourself against a sky bright and bloody

to bathe yourself in light   & go back to the old world   a brand-new inflection

migración

a 'germination' is a poetic form invented
by Natalie Linh Bolderston

papá	holds	waiting
head whirling	some language	on that plane
now oceans away	under the tongue	those new horizons
there	through /	here
luciérnagas blush	alongside / between	titiwai beading
archways of goodbyes	each tangled pathway	fish-lines into clay
flies	slowly	home
from méxico	to aotearoa	his hands
like orange butterflies	riding the clouds	always so warm
outer	years	fell
landscapes bent	like birds	into wind
to inner ones	gesturing towards change	a quiet movement

photograph

here everything remains / in a time before destiny /
before flinching / when the sun was horizontal / getting louder /
collision imminent / you the conducting rod /
in a red coat / arms against the blue / setting the view loose /
the sum of your parts / an index / the lick of a thumb /
the sealing of a letter / thrown into a wind / before wind

apple tree bay

we sleep with our heads on a ribbon of dune
between two pieces of sea
drifting into corridors of sound, sand
the wet blue grasses
of the unknown ocean
our bodies pumping blood
                      back and forth
                            like the tide

                                jellyfish filter through silica &
                                    into our sleep-visions
                                      pulse red and nebular
                            filled with no thought but the water
                                    hollow like boats
                                          strung up
                                            above
                                      the drift

elsewhere   three kōkopu
– shapes of spirit – move
through portals between worlds
elsewhere   a child
is born into the wetland
lines of silver run
                down their mother's legs
                            into the sea

                          your breath folds itself outwards
                  you reach towards me in the gathering light
                        the whole beach is in your fingernails
                                & in the morning
                            we wring out the towels
                                  the tent still
                                damp
                            from dreaming

two trees

tomorrow she walks in
and then it's yesterday again
and this time she doesn't fall.
tomorrow
she will see the gaps in the
floorboards and then yesterday
she will step aside to leave
the mouth of dark
to itself.

are you there? she whispers and
the mouth is open but
doesn't speak. wind sings
coins out of the sky.
the tomorrow-that-is-yesterday
blankets the walls.
apples sweeten in the hidden
places behind windows.

the pool
    a golden shovel poem after H.D.

tell me what you are
soft-bodied heavy on the clay you
shake silt making it silver crumbling it alive

on the surface and then under i
look wide-eyed waiting to touch
the silent shine inside you

where two currents shift you
meet me there blushing to quiver
around the curve of my hand like
wind over rock like the moon ghosts a
circle around the shadows of sea-fish

my back arched upwards i
reach out fingers to cover
the space above you
shield your eyes from the sun with
gaps between to find you in my
ropes of memory later in my dreaming net

so tell me what
unknown world   what love of mine are
              you –
in what futures have we found each other & banded
into one?

as inside as the eye can see
in response to artwork by Casilda Sánchez

all
       compressed distance

all   static   at once

wave and particle   your

     space(unspecified)

too close   by half

or was it   not close enough

so much sight or is it

    no sight at all

air exchanged
     above the rim   (eyelid,
                                      anemone)

hours loosening   to seconds
     forgotten visions

almost   restored

O fill my empty looking

     162. with what eyes?

with yours

     45. as long as you want
     163. my darling one

particles

people are lighting small fires on our beach & the smoke rises
up to join the sea-mist, which moves in steady
screens across the water, apricot coloured,
& the waves gust towards us in great unrelenting
blocks, square-edged, like they're computer-generated,
& children run into them, unafraid, tossing kelp
over their shoulders like satchels,
& people walk in pairs through the filtered light, & i think
of you in our brand-new room, of our clothes
wrapped up together in the drawers & of the little lists
we wrote, nail up the shelf, vacuum behind the bed,
& of the tide pool filling up in front of me, &
all this new time pouring in through my sides –
                                            & how   at home you are waiting for me –
& how   clinging to the dream-substrate

we will sleep together again, tonight –

| **soaring asleep** | **falling awake** |

we approach the subduction zone   underneath the earth gathering
smile   flinty   warm with change   sliding on hinges of shadow

night twists downward like   a magnolia tree   curls into its dreams
   lava moves into oceans   the moon slews itself   away to the south

fire folding   into discovery   the sea ice sluicing into the water

& something   a flood of silver
   pulls me onwards   waiting for tomorrow   & each day
         circling   I wake up to the same bellbird
            sounding out

through different kinds

of light   the morning

omens

The night before moving is clear & the stars
cobweb through the glass with the streetlight.
The pear tree is quiet still & full of fruit,
its leaves like paper cranes half-folded in their sleep

& the window is open – enough for some sky to spill inwards
with a coolness that flows over my arms
and Ru beside me who murmurs and sighs,
his closed eyes half-moons in the pillow-dark.

The more I remember time the more I press my face to the glass of it
the more the outside world seems to vibrate with memory
of its own. It whispers through the window's mouth &
in a language I half-understand says *look*,

look through the cob-light at your hand
at the border of yourself, at the center of the eyeline,
at the dust coming away. *Look*, a tomorrow
many years from now maybe – the same hand

with more story in it – the pears ripe again on the grass – the dog
or the ghost eating them – each bedroom you sleep in will place
a new window in your memory – each night will sing you
the same song in a different voice –

J. A. Vili

Poems Lost During the Void

Funding Cuts Deep
   for Tui

Jazz Thornton's on the news this morning

is there another girl
on another bridge?

contemplating gods & flying lessons

with fractured wings
& broken wairua

catching rays & stinging barbs – carving

poems into wrists – kōrero
smoke into ambiguous eyes

of the vulnerable – the queenless beehive

cuts funding to govern –
mental states

disregard the contagion & torrent times

tāngata dissent – climbing
the branches of the kōwhai

the tūī – sing in protest.

Carnival at the Point
    for Jaguar

Our boy doesn't remember you
only from old photographs
none that show you holding him
well, not in your arms

there's a polaroid of a mini-train ride
where our boy sits in the middle carriage
between you & his sister, he doesn't know
we were celebrating his second birthday

now he tells me a story about alpacas
walking past Point England Reserve
& a pretty lady is holding the reins
guiding them to shade under an old pine

then I remember the Gypsy carnival
a year after the new millennium
travellers from the South Island, I heard
setting up their caravans by Tahuna Torea

the posters over the graffitied walls
invite the community to join their festivities
experience their nomadic way of life
their smiles full of pastoral humility

you could feel their closeness
how they spoke their own language
kept warm eyes over their visitors
treating the children like their own

I was at ease in their presence
felt their neighbourly warmth
admired their rustic arts and crafts
showing traces of their wanderlust

I remember you won a raffle that day
that I bought a carved smoking pipe
how we both gapped it past the fortune teller
taking our girl to the pony rides

did I tell our boy this story before?
make it sound so biblical, so memorable
how else could he remember that day?
I know he was not there

I can hear boxes falling from my room
I don't know why he is so angry
then silence, as he returns to the lounge
'I told you I was there, Dad.'

he shows me an old photograph
I still don't understand
then he points to your image
& then I see your swollen belly

I don't know whether to laugh or cry
but I see how much it means to him
I tell him the photo proves he was right
as he buries his taonga into his chest.

Tulip Season
    for the Hill family

Estuaries rupture the mountain's spleen
Angus tongues are lapping the boundary creek
where an abandoned hīnaki is trapping waste
the old man ridicules the imminent rain, forecasted
he cuts through the rib cage of the gorge
sliding down past the crimson braids of tea-tree
ready for the trailer, he is tracking by stomach
& his bow is too far away – he is slipping

the deer are too fast on the shingled ridges
so he sidetracks down the radiata valley
listening to the boom of the steel log trucks
splitting down the fringe of the muddy basin
he catches his mate's bike heading to the house
along the hill where his wife used to plant tulips
they haven't flowered since her departure
it's that landscape that turns into abstract smudge

Jorja is picking wild flowers with Russell, the Lab
sniffing at the pūkeko straying from the wetlands
the last of summer's corn being eaten by the goats
shows how wet the season was, flood-wet, wet-wet
little Piper is swinging in the hammock on the porch
& Evil is lurking by the new chicken coop again
last week, Dad crumbled some of Nana's rock cakes
over the veggie garden, haven't seen a rabbit since

Matiu is here to fix the black ute again, Old Buck
named after the All Black, cause he always gets back up
& Dad says, there's a loose nut down in the engine
back with no bow, cursing the ear-splitting trucks
scaring tonight's dinner away, well that's his excuse
Evil & the girls run up, show him the messy flowers
hoping the trip is still on, weather-wise & car-wise
the girls aren't as timid anymore, slowly healing

Evil has already bagged Mum's seat, he knows
she was his mum too, I put him on my lap
Jorja & Piper in the back seat, vibing out to Lorde
Matiu is leaving with a case of Dad's home brew
I'm pretty sure Dad only makes it to pay for car repairs
now I know, Matiu will never tighten that loose nut
Dad's a vaper now, vibing out on orchard fruits
driving past the piled slash, we enter the iron gates

some tulip bulbs have shot through, by Emma's stone
the girls are quiet, a smile sprouts from Dad's face
I can see the clouds lifting over the chapel roof
& that stupid cat trying to lock the car door again
buses of new fruit pickers at Mac's orchard arrive
next door to the quarry, still covered in sediment
at least the floods never reached the cemetery
& the girls don't cry anymore, when we visit.

Strategic Manoeuvres
    for Mr and Mrs Ioane

It's the fraudulent voice that finds you
when you lose your brothers to the sea
maybe it's the ocean in both your ears
that balances the weight of your glitch
or that friend who was, now antagonising
when you cut ties to find your meaning

bonded over detention in the school library
played chess with her, while I read poetry
note your Casio watch that always told 3:33
every time Mrs Jones popped out for a ciggie
might be telling us something else
maybe it's time to get a life . . . or nine

the first move sets you up – check yourself
losing all your men, just for your infatuation
our dance-floor battles were getting old
& we couldn't remember much from that night
or how the shrimp got into the tequila bottle
but you did bring her to the school ball

it's the coin toss of your Druid penny
that flipped us off, when you gave it to her
the protective knight she found in you
made us realise, you were in a Siberian Trap
your rookie moves made us laugh
but it's all fair in love & war games

gave her your complete surrender – your capture
before she introduced you to her family & friends
the future shifted the loss of your brothers
countered – by the terminal growth in her neck
not that guests thought your wedding was dark
but your heartfelt vows brightened the mood

'It's about losing & finding new family', that got us
so we cleared the board & guarded her till the end
but you never see those deceptive traps ahead
God's pretextual move, that takes your queen away
I'm not worried about the games we played
I'm just here to check on you, mate.

Tobruk Road
    for Iuni

Between Tripoli and Dunkirk, the horizon has changed forever
bull tanks eat asbestos, wrecking old pipes and friendships
new roots hide grapefruit traps under damp cypress leaves
but you can still take the shortcut through Sollum or Derna
if old neighbours are still alive, new fences bring new faces
& past wars are remembered, honoured and paraded

the corrugated plum tree hid my secrets in her crevices
my father's taro patch, camouflaged an army of street kids
our shed, my concrete bunker surrounded by an onion mine
with the old trellis of tamarillos, my wall of defence
from the blitz of monkey apples and Chilean guavas
followed by a barrage of rotten apples and sibling rivalry

my brave sisters are trying to outflank me from the ground
one plays on weekends for her softball club – short stop
the other, on the bench for her school rugby team – short fuse
both now emerging out of the bean tunnels, target locked
my feijoa grenades aimed thirty degrees from a vantage point
I was an expert at quantum warfare & bullshit back then

back, when the weather and crescent tides were predictable
& the mountains never woke up spewing their anger
when April was still humid and burning scars from a Cuban sun
when May was still warm like the tepid pools behind St Mary's
& June was still giving me the cold shoulder from her balcony
back, when we fought wars with fruit & loved the enemy next door.

Under the Willows of Maybury
for Saia

Bruh, been thinking about you this week
your team got knocked out again
probably see you first, before they win a final
but I'll have one for you, if they ever do

saw your old lady outside gardening again

those delinquent years at your house
from boys to men & back to boys again
catching rides with your old man
to watch the Warriors, play touch

I'm just fucking with you, Bruh

I was down at the library yesterday
that's why you popped up in my head
the tree that displays your cross
was freshly dressed with orange flowers

just like the ones in your mum's garden

anyways, grabbed us a bottle for a catch-up
going to our refuge, through the old reserve
where we used to hide from the teachers
& where I met your sister for the first time

the place hasn't changed that much

the crippled willows, still offering shelter
now hollowed out by the old feral creek
Cheers Bruh, here's to next season
I still come to our old hideout, now & then

It's where I keep your shadow.

Jaywalking a Turtle
for Tomas

I can't tell you that I was walking my pet turtle
through a festive Queen Street on St Patrick's Day
although that would have been a cool night
paint a shamrock on its shell & call him Kinsella
after the poet, feed it clover from Albert Park
& do an Irish pub crawl, no whiskey of course
just a saucer of Guinness at the Shakespeare Tavern
but you couldn't give Kinsey too much, he'll snap

Turtle was the name we called our workmate
fresh off a fishing boat from the Philippines
here for repairs & to visit family I knew
his English was good, due to karaoke rock classics
catch him saying song lyrics to you in conversation
then look at each other thinking, is he trying to sing
or is he just quoting Robert Plant to you
cause you know, words can have two meanings

we kit him out in a Celtics singlet & green bandana
exit our hotel on Customs, go through Fort to Queen
he keeps asking if they sell San Miguel beer here
not tonight, my kaibigan, tonight we drown in nectar
a five-foot-two fisherman out of water, his stories grow
like the fish he caught after each death-defying trawl
double-dribbling Irish cream, laying-up shots of Jameson's
the locals love him, even more after singing U2 songs

have to call it a night & take our half-naked friend home
give every man his due, just not Tullamore Dew
we have to return Turtle back to the water tomorrow
to help his crew finish water blasting the mollusc hull
heading down Victoria to Queen, commotion on Elliott
waves of chanting green overlapping the blue line
a group of medieval partygoers being questioned
jump off the stairs, a hot pursuit is in progress

there's an athletic man rocking a leprechaun mask
hurdling park benches & being chased by the po-po
screaming like a banshee through the Atrium plaza
late shoppers scatter, but the pigeons hold their line
the guy manages to throw in some Riverdance moves
before getting cuffed outside the Stables – good times
we stop to rest outside the public library, light up
& take in some Robert Sullivan poetry to wind down

just heard from his uncle that Turtle had passed last year
doing what he loved, I'd like to say it was karaoke
but that was the nature of the man, trawling up friends
at different ports around the Pacific, singing praises
from people he met at bars and new fans at O'Hagan's
'You know they're from an island too, like us', he'd say
bummed out now, going to lay up some shots at the local
long overdue for a Tullamore & one for my kaibigan.

Moonwalker
    for Samuelu

you & your glass pipe dreams
fading away like the smoke trails from a shuttle
your room, covered in maps of astrology and tides
I remember how much you loved that big poster
full of destinations & dreamscapes few have been
how you wanted to swim in the Sea of Tranquility
that you would be the first in your family to visit
not realising that you would be the first human

you were dumb like that
but that just made your impossible – possible

you & your glass pipe dreams
phasing your passage through the steps of recovery
Hevelius tries to guide your oblique sunlight
away from the moon's dark side – eclipsing
your former self, as you prepare to crash-land
now you remember 'Letters to a Young Poet'
as you drown in Lacus Mortis, facing the Woolf
Lunar, your co-pilot can howl from the moon

you were dumb like that
but that just made your independence – dependent

you & your glass pipe dreams
disturbing your thoughts – you start losing gravity
as you quote scripture from the Book of Ruth
while you drift over the ridges of Montes Recti
summon Zion & shout out verses from Obadiah
when you reach the summit of Mons Pico
tell me how you would build a greater wall
from moon rocks, so we could see it from Earth

you were dumb like that
but that just made your ethereal – real

Never thought you would launch early,
I'm fucking dumb for that.

At the Feet of a Mountain
    for Betty

Her head carved by surgeons
scars the ridge of her crown
a smile down one cheek
buried under layered skin
shows her spirit at its peak

she sings her waiata to her husband
still untouched by the cold
he knows she is frail
but she still holds her whānau
to her chest, as always

the path is paved for her return
home to her maunga
whānau and friends circle her bed
gathering debris, falling
from her crumbling temple

Taranaki waits for his disciple
the woman who left years ago
will be at his feet again
when the snow finds her at rest
may it cover her with peace

Beside His Mountain
    for Rangi

Her waiata stirs his sleep
warns him of the oncoming cold
his mountain view eclipsed
a new dawn, fresh with season
warms his memories of her

haere mai, haere mai
his token heart invites
one and all, everything
his whare welcomes
all our differences

he stirs a fusion of cultures
his recipe for harmony
kai for his manuhiri
feeds the people with kindness
until they are full with friendship

the cold has found him
but God did not call his name
followed his wife's waiata to the grave
he now lies beside his maunga
her snow has finally arrived

Sleeping with Bats
    for Tafa

She is not accustomed to signals given by men
the tat-tattoo-ing of the bone combing skin
she knows the purity of her canvas has been baptised
in the name of the Father, her father & the one upstairs
sings a psalm instead of prayer, she is flying blind
her blood is dark now – lost its virtue
but she doesn't cry or weep like her wounds

opens the bamboo shade of Jesus in mildew – branded
in her sleep, she puts on her Karen Walker glasses
splintered & pre-loved, just like her former shell
post-damaged, she flies out the door in heels-high
last gulp of rosé to kill the tablets – she dissolves
into the streets of 'Old Pap', on princess mode
but she doesn't cry or tear up like her ripped jeans –

stumbles to her silence through the mangroves
to the big pipe over the mudflats, behind the village
if her father was still alive, the one upstairs
would be on his radar – hunted & wings clipped
she touches the pride on her arm, before she sleeps
no more transgressions between blood & church
a two-faced bat flies upstairs, back to its dark shame.

Passage Southside

The broken letterbox talks to me in tongues
I try to read the broken lips of the bottles
scuffing the edges of my blue bin
Byrd barks at the new neighbours
hushing traffic past the playground

dodge the buses aligned with artists
on their way to create origins of design
to paint the world in reverse sepia
the markets are slow, winding down
but I catch the last punnet of mussels

time to suit up for another memorial
for another elder, dropping like flies
since the lockdowns released sceptics
& calls of deceit, it's just politics
my black tie has lost its colour & faith

the new off-ramps, off-putting the eyes
& Manukau seems to be growing upwards
into fake skylines, burning rubber into clouds
my third visit this year, another on the way
damn, these gardens are getting popular.

My Chemical Break Up
for Ravyn

I am in her black book, which used to be a good thing
make-up all over the zodiac-signed pillows – fading
& her artwork on the floor, splattered with hues of frustration
the frenzied portraits blur melting hibiscus with silent screams
I am recovering today, can't be in two minds at the same time
she's trying to find answers, but her mum's vessel has sailed
at Hell Pizza, she orders wrath & purgatory – I'm done!
what's the worst that I can say, I just play our song

she was kinder then, before the repercussion of hollow drums
had her marching to a different beat – tongue tripping slurs
a Bohemia of buskers humming Buddha chants – melancholy
mantra of reincarnation to reality – still thinks she's in control
I am in trouble today, trying to flounder under the clouds
now her worn Chucks are ripping holes in her story threads
the metal studs binding words she wrote to me once, in Gaelic
what's the worst that I can say, I just play our song

she didn't have to go out that way, comatose on expectations
tartan skirts, MCR t-shirts & demons in the high-lands
heard her whisper a poem by Carol Ann Duffy one night
girl in a red hat with young aspirations, being eaten by a wolf
I am mourning today, black on black, nails & all – fuck it!
walking up to her grave, I take her poem from my pocket
what's the worst that I can say, I just play dead & whisper
the last lines of our song, so long & goodnight . . .

Flutter
    for Angela M

some people shine light, opalescent
through ancient kauri shimmering frogs
dry leaves past the bank, race over stones
cradling your paper boat in the pool
of spinning mosquitos, catching your web
& your wings flutter, between brook & cascade

the heat of the blurring asphalt
melts your sticky Trumpet wrapper
slipping off the cheeky monkey bars
the house keys catch you falling
into hysterical laughter, after the f word
& your wings flutter, between swing & slide

you tell me to follow, before your father returns
taking me to the dark comfort of his den
you hand me your favourite poetry book
cigar-cut open to verses from an old poet
the banker's lamp flickers your light, perfectly
& your wings flutter, between vinyls & paperbacks

your casket covered with synthetic butterflies
that you collected with albums & boyfriends
I wanted to read you a poem from the book
but I didn't want your father to see it in my hands
not in the same hands that held his daughter
& now your wings flutter, between chrysalis & flight.

Returning a Gift
for Whetu P

coasting the 756 to the ports, where her son used to work
time off work for another tangi – another poem to bury
can't face machines or high ceilings today, or the next
i catch the boats praying to the mongers at the viaduct
trying to inflate lungs from sucking up salt at the markets
& the burning ice on hooks melting the fish guts away

the walk is short, spirits are high for such a sad occasion
looks like he was well liked by his work colleagues
i reminisce watching him grow up in the local hoods
buying his third guitar & taking him fishing on the pier
how he became friends with the melting pot of faces
down at the wharf, who only knew his friendly nature

you never see the dark clouds coming, even in waves
from around the whenua, over the transcendent maunga
down the fossil driveways – into your once-safe spaces
give it shelter to intensify, while it gnaws at your wairua
biting on your conscience, as your nothingness escalates
tide after tide, stone after stone – drowning under the weight

i see his forever mother already weaving people together
calling her tūpuna to welcome her only child, gifted to her
she couldn't stop the shadows carving out his light
whānau radiate stories about a musician, a fisherman,
a gentle joker & his haerenga with his doting mother
the rain has made her silent, masking her tears

his pounamu pick had frayed the copper strings of Jimi
he had a habit of naming his belongings, some lost
from foster home, to foster home; to kainga
from foster mum, to foster mum; to tina
forget all their names, except for the one he belonged to
the rain has stopped, her tears transparent.

Mother's Rope

you lock the door
within

take your seat
standing up

head down low
your shadow hangs high

the rope
like your mother's cord

you take
for granted

the maternal bond
you forget

she is forever
tied to you

& if you jump
a mother dies too.

Road Trip to Kaipara
    for Chelz & Benz

It's a long way to go for a rugby league game
car radio can't tune into Hēnare's frequency
of rolling numbers & Capstan tobacco cigarettes
coughing up crabs till your throat burns zodiac
channel into Sora's static barking in the back
& Suki's ears catching waves outside the window

Warehouse bargains litter the boot – unopened
& the chilly bin's still on Christmas mode
switch to CD, cause tradition plays centre
when karakia is needed for a safe journey
'Back in Black', revs the wagon up – Amen
kick-off & we chase the motorway out west

tap Ben's head twice – he's used to that now
it's the echo he hears, not the first whistle
he turns & feeds the backs with cans of L&P
or as Hēnare called them, lemon & pineapple
we never let him forget that day – the drop kick
cause we all know; they only grow lemons in Paeroa

trip's kicking in & Ben's munching on rainbows
the sugary kind, Chelsea snaps awake again
back on autopilot, cause it's past noonish
& she had Bernadino all night & for brekky
she thinks it's still Friday, bubbles are bursting
finds her centre when she spots the Waitākeres

she's a Westie, face leathered by the black sands
& blood laced with motorcycle fuel – her take
met her at the lion's feet, during the last Matariki
likes to moon-travel, no parachute – interstellar
wears a bead necklace with her mum's ashes
fossilised in dragon-blood resin, fused to her heart

she triple-taps her cousin Ben's head & he's crying foul
the second echo hurt, Chelsea scores for the ladies
toilet stop for the dogs. 'For Sora & Suki too', she yells
Chelsea's game is on fire, she thinks a hat trick is due
there's four bottles of 'Bern' left in the chilly bin
she's feeling offside, the next café calls – half time

staring at a wagon wheel under a tree in Taupaki
rolling herbs in thyme & parsley wheeling extract
a goat that looks like Hēnare has got the munchies too
in a paddock full of emeralds, poor Chelsea's clover
it's the simple things that make her rich – her take
back on the road revving up another AC/DC track

we never made it to the game that day – my take
called into Kumeū Cemetery, to toast Chelsea's dad
but as soon as her tears started flowing – game over
our team can cope with our absence, the impassive loss
our constant supporter hasn't been coping well this season
so we stayed, huddled around her & 'Berned' the day away.

Ashes of Atticus
    for my niece

I still dream of you, buried
under coliseums in ruin
like the Roman librarian
who bled for his literature

your memoirs unwritten
Julius arrives for mourning
your father came from the West
to set the East on fire

in the core of Chantelle
you lived & died, unborn
casting a shadow over us
tears would not find your grave

your name echoed hope
ignored by the immortals
with your impending life
still revered in the present

we gathered to feast
in your timeless memory
honour you with the promise
of what could have been

I see a vessel blessed
by a colony of church bats
ready to carry your ashes
towards the missionary shore

but today the wind passed you by
you must take another road home
find your great-grandfather's grave
& return to your ancient gods

I could see the memorial gardens
in full bloom with vivid flags
draped over statuette angel wings
& your urn, resting on Taelega's stone.

Ōrākei Sunset
    for Jaguar

today, I gave and received
zodiac oa, bought by a father
a fish head – harpoon tail – symbol
Tagaloa heads the table
exalting
praise for a son's tausamiga

stone washed – tortoise shell – face
watching his tinamatua kneel
Manuia lou aso fanau
a tribute is offered to Le Atua
revelling
four years awake

shags relish the fresh fish
tame birds – feral skies – farewell
the outgoing tide of 'aiga
leaving with a goddess
waving
her brother goodnight

across from an old Māori cemetery
the outfitted boats – wet bathers – rowdy
I am witness to the fortune
of the illuminated trees
blooming in,
over
Ōkahu.

Whangaparāoa Sunrise
for Athena

today, I lost and found
washed-up taonga, gathered by a father
a fish tail – harpoon head – token
Tangaroa heads the table
blessing
grace for a daughter's hākari

sand-dyed – polished pāua – face
watching her kuia kneel
Hari rā whānau ki a koe
a toast is raised to Te Atua
rejoicing
sixteen years awake

seagulls ravage the dead eels
feral birds – tame skies – welcome
the incoming tide of whānau
arriving with a chief
greeting
his sister good morning

across from an old soldiers' camp
the naked shore – burnt coast – silent
I am witness to the tragedy
of the wounded trees
bleeding out,
over
Shakespear.

Not for the Young
for my children

the night crashes my sleep with a knock on the door
apologies torch the carpet with their tipsy feet
there's a crisis, not meant for children's hearts
they are too pure to comprehend bereavement
so my mind absorbs what memories they have
& how do I carry them through this winter storm
I brace my warm coat, as if it had your pulse
& I wonder, what do I tell them?

the car is full, the lights cutting the brakes
on the dark gathering, ahead of the sirens
there's a scene, not meant for children's eyes
they are too young to recognise real trauma
so my instinct is to summon family to prepare
news travels fast through the asphalt sticks
I brace my phone, as if I would hear your voice
& I wonder, how do I tell them?

the tree untouched, the metal carcass warped
peace sits under the branches with frail faces
there's a conversation, not meant for children's ears
they are too innocent to understand true grief
so my thoughts are trying to find accountability
the first responders let me through the tape
I brace my hands, as if they were yours
& I wonder, when do I tell them?

you are cold, as if peace was sacrificed for you
& the damp room, finding fault with my disposition
there's a place, not meant for children's presence
they are too naïve to acknowledge finality
so my reflections find no answers for my resolve
I brace myself, as if I had your adversity
& I wonder, if tomorrow I will find the courage.

My Greatest Poems
    for my children

one lost agaga

I can light the fire of Le Pasefika
guide you to your tuaa

weave a pattern of flames
back to the beginning

carve your grand paopao
for your malaga

but that is yours to ignite,
yours to unravel
& yours to explore

    I am not a poem like you   I just create them.

one wairua lost

   she can stir the waters of Te Moana-nui-a-Kiwa
   guide you to your tūpuna

   weave a pattern of tides
   back to the beginning

   carve your glorious waka
   for your haerenga

   but that is yours to incite,
   yours to untangle
   & yours to discover

    She is not a poem like you   she just gives them life.

Your Tangi
    for your tamariki

Tears falling in Kaikohe
find passage downstream
over riverstone altars that
bless the feet of mountains
Beauty of untouched forest
I see beyond mellow fields
Your aunties tell me   you
would gather watercress there

Hot pools spray mist
over the crest of your marae
Your brothers stand stoic
as the cemetery walls
that guard your mother
The chapel tolls waiata
with your sons' voices
resonating in karakia

Under Ngāwhā skies
of cloudy pastures
I stand above   you
tending to our trees
Our girl weeps beside me
watching you descend
She knows   you
will not return

Our boy in his suit
kneels on the mound
ushering the earth
onto your vessel
He lies on his back
making earth angels
Whānau are amused.
'That's his Hāmoa side.'

A man with a shovel
looks annoyed and
walks towards our boy
'Let him bury his mother.'
I say with alofa
His eyes acknowledge
with surprise – then sadness
as he strokes our boy's face

Our girl stands still
on the edge of your grave
Her tears fall in hymn
with the returning soil
Our boy joins his brothers
to challenge the gods
with your haka.
He is laughing with the sun

'Is Mummy sleeping, Daddy?'
He does not know   you
will not return
Our girl now stirs
'No. She's dead, aye Daddy?'
Trying to stem their tears
they wait for my answer
to comfort their hearts

But I am carved in thought
My tongue is kauri
My eyes are shells
My heart is stone
In a graveyard sowed with death
I am captured –
by how full of life
the weeds are.

Notes

Arcadiana

'The Apotheosis of Captain Cook, 20 January 1794', Royal Academy of Arts, www.royalacademy.org.uk/art-artists/work-of-art/the-apotheosis-of-captain-cook

'Arcadiana string quartet', Faber Music, www.fabermusic.com/music/arcadiana-2365

'Between the Covers Teju Cole Interview', *Tin House*, 16 February 2021, https://tinhouse.com/transcript/between-the-covers-teju-cole-interview

Calvino, Italo, *Invisible Cities*, Vintage, 1997.

Druett, Joan, 'Tupaia, Chief Mourner painting', Te Ara Encyclopedia of New Zealand, 12 September 2018, https://teara.govt.nz/en/artwork/46864/chief-mourner-painting

Fresno State Mfa, 'Fresno Poets Archive 12 – Li-Young Lee', YouTube, www.youtube.com/watch?v=hApa0-Yep24&ab_channel=FresnoStateMfa

Grimm, Jacob and Wilhelm, *The Juniper Tree*, https://sites.pitt.edu/~dash/grimm047.html

The Holy Bible, www.biblegateway.com

katabasis, 'do you guys think jesus …', Tumblr, 7 December 2023, www.tumblr.com/katabasiss/735986907117469696/do-you-guys-think-jesus-the-son-of-a-carpenter

Kozinn, Allan, 'Quartet Embraces the New and the Slightly Less New', *New York Times*, 19 February 1999, www.nytimes.com/1999/02/19/movies/music-review-quartet-embraces-the-new-and-the-slightly-less-new.html

noknowshame, 'why is religious Christmas imagery all so joyful and pleasant …', Tumblr, 1 December 2023, www.tumblr.com/noknowshame/735543568333160448/noknowshame-why-is-religious-christmas-imagery

Obeyesekere, Gananath, *The Apotheosis of Captain Cook: European Mythmaking in the Pacific*, Princeton University, 1997.

Rose, Deborah Bird, and Debbie Bird Rose, 'Worshipping Captain Cook', *Social Analysis: The International Journal of Social and Cultural Practice*, no. 34 (1993): 43–49, www.jstor.org/stable/23163005

Seneca, Lucius, and John D'Agata, 'Sick', *Conjunctions*, no. 51 (2008): 69–70, www.jstor.org/stable/24517525

Somoff, Victoria, 'On the Metahistorical Roots of the Fairytale', *Western Folklore* 61, no. 3/4 (2002): 277–93, https://doi.org/10.2307/1500423

Stepniak, Michael, and Peter Sirotin, *Beyond the Conservatory Model: Reimagining Classical Music Performance Training in Higher Education*, Routledge, 2021.

Subin, Anna Della, *Accidental Gods: On Men Unwittingly Turned Divine*, Granta, 2022.

Te Punga Somerville, Alice, *Two Hundred and Fifty Ways to Start an Essay about Captain Cook*, Bridget Williams Books, 2020.

Whitman, John, *Snow White and the Seven Dwarfs*, Funtastic, 2005.

intertidal
'trace fossils' and 'two trees' first appeared in *Starling* 15, 'sappho 21' and 'apple tree bay' in *Starling* 16, 'only' and 'particles' in *Sweet Mammalian* 10, and 'lift / up / over / sounding' and 'where will the spirits live' in *Minarets* 14.

The glosa 'bajo la luna, un caballo de noche' contains lines from Louise Glück's poem 'Omens', first published in her tenth poetry collection *Averno* (Farrar, Straus and Giroux, 2006).

Poems Lost During the Void
'Mother's Rope' and 'Your Tangi' first appeared in *Ika* 3. 'Your Tangi' was published in *Katūivei: Contemporary Pasifika Poetry from Aotearoa New Zealand*, edited by David Eggleton, Vaughan Rapatahana and Mere Taito (Massey University Press, 2024).

Xiaole Zhan (詹小乐) is a Chinese-New Zealand writer and composer based in Naarm. They are the recipient of the 2024 Kat Muscat Fellowship. Awards include the *Kill Your Darlings* Creative Non-Fiction Essay Prize and the Charles Brasch Young Writers' Essay Competition. Their work has appeared in *Island*, *The Suburban Review*, *Landfall*, *Cordite Poetry Review*, *Going Down Swinging*, *Starling* and *Sweet Mammalian*. Their name in Chinese is 小乐 and means 'Little Happy' but can also be read as 'Little Music'.

Margo Montes de Oca is a poet and researcher of Mexican and Pākehā descent living in Te Whanganui-a-Tara. She holds degrees in English literature and in ecology and biodiversity. She was a 2024 *Starling* writer-in-residence at the New Zealand Young Writers Festival, and her poetry has been published in issues of *Starling*, *Sweet Mammalian*, *bad apple*, *Minarets* and *Mayhem Literary Journal*.

J. A. Vili is an Auckland-based poet of Samoan descent whose poetry often advocates for suicide prevention and mental illness support. He dedicates poems to friends and to his children who lost their mother at a young age. Vili holds a bachelor of creative writing. His poems have appeared in *Ika* journal and *Katūīvei: Contemporary Pasifika Poetry from Aotearoa New Zealand* (Massey University Press, 2024).

First published 2025
Auckland University Press
Waipapa Taumata Rau
University of Auckland
Private Bag 92019
Auckland 1142
New Zealand
www.aucklanduniversitypress.co.nz

© Xiaole Zhan, Margo Montes de Oca, J. A. Vili, 2025

ISBN 978 1 77671 171 0

A catalogue record for this book is available from the National Library of New Zealand

This book is copyright. Apart from fair dealing for the purpose of private study, research, criticism or review, as permitted under the Copyright Act, no part may be reproduced by any process without prior permission of the publisher. The moral rights of the authors have been asserted.

Every effort has been made to trace copyright holders and obtain permission to reproduce copyright material.

Design by Greg Simpson
This book was printed on FSC® certified paper
Printed in Singapore by Markono Print Media Pte Ltd